# 24 Day

## Recipe Collection

Assembled by Independent AdvoCare Distributors

This collection on recipes has been assembled and published by Independent AdvoCare Distributors and is not provided by, endorsed by or affiliated with AdvoCare International, L.P.

*Freedom Beach*

ISBN-13: 978-0615787510
ISBN-10: 0615787517

# Contents

**Main Dishes** ............................................................................. 7

    Asian Chicken Stir Fry ........................................................ 8

    Moroccan Chicken with Fruit Topping ........................... 9

    Applesauce Chicken ......................................................... 10

    Chicken Azteca ................................................................. 11

    Chicken Fajitas ................................................................. 12

    Chicken Burritos .............................................................. 13

    Chicken and Spinach Skillet Dish .................................. 14

    Mediterranean Chicken ................................................... 15

    Savory Moroccan Chicken .............................................. 16

    Winter Chicken Bake ....................................................... 18

    Hungarian Chicken .......................................................... 19

    Spaghetti ........................................................................... 20

    Pasta .................................................................................. 21

    Tuna ................................................................................... 22

    Zesty Tuna ........................................................................ 23

    Chili .................................................................................... 24

    Tex/Mex Chili ................................................................... 25

    Meatloaf ............................................................................ 26

    Asian Lettuce Wraps ....................................................... 27

    Zesty Chicken Marinade ................................................. 28

    Grilled Cajun Chicken ..................................................... 29

    Terrific Grilled Chicken ................................................... 30

    Grilled Lemon Chicken ................................................... 31

    Grilled Caribbean Chicken ............................................. 32

    Zesty Bun-less Burgers ................................................... 33

    Bun-less Burgers .............................................................. 34

Hawaiian Bun-less Burgers ...................................................35

Black Beans and Rice ........................................................36

Baked Tilapia ................................................................37

BBQ Chicken..................................................................38

Frijoles Cubanos.............................................................39

Saucy Salmon ...............................................................40

Lean and Spicy Taco Meat ...................................................42

Grilled Basil-Marinated Chicken ............................................43

Salmon .....................................................................44

Country Captain Slow Cooker Chicken ........................................45

Marmalade Curry Chicken ....................................................46

Turkey with Mango Salsa ....................................................47

Warm Pineapple and Chicken Salad ...........................................48

Slow Cooked Rice and Chicken ...............................................49

Curried Chicken with Pineapple..............................................50

Caribbean Fish .............................................................51

Black Bean- Mango Salsa Wrap ...............................................52

Veggie Packed Sloppy Joe's .................................................53

Sweet Potato Lasagna........................................................54

Grilled Tuna Steak..........................................................56

Mediterranean Stuffed Peppers ..............................................57

Indian Spiced Chicken and Lentils...........................................58

Chicken and Eggplant........................................................59

Chicken and Avocado Salad ..................................................60

Baked Tilapia with Dill Sauce ..............................................61

Stuffed Red Peppers ........................................................62

Easy Tofu (Or Chicken) Stir Fry.............................................63

Almond Butter Chili ........................................................64

Sweet Potato Chili..........................................................65

*Side Dishes*................................................................................... 67

    Spinach Deviled Eggs .......................................................... 68

    Ratatouille .............................................................................. 69

    Roasted Vegetables ............................................................. 70

    Tex-Mex Rice ........................................................................ 71

    Spanish Rice ......................................................................... 72

    Pineapple Brown Rice ......................................................... 73

    Sweet Potato Fries .............................................................. 74

    Savory Couscous................................................................... 75

    Sweet and Nutty Moroccan Couscous .............................. 76

    Couscous with Dried Fruit ................................................. 77

    Roasted Asparagus with Pine Nuts................................... 78

    Quick Pasta-Veggie Medley................................................ 79

    Barley with Kalamata Olives and Tomatoes..................... 80

    Peanut Noodle Salad .......................................................... 81

    Veggie Quinoa Salad........................................................... 82

*Miscellaneous*............................................................................. 83

    Garlic Dressing..................................................................... 84

    Homemade Taco Seasoning ............................................... 85

    Pam's Chicken Baste........................................................... 86

    Strawberry Jello................................................................... 87

    Tofu sour cream .................................................................. 88

*Shopping Guidelines* .................................................................. 89

# Main Dishes

# Asian Chicken Stir Fry

- ½ teaspoon powdered ginger
- ¼ teaspoon garlic powder
- 2 tablespoons Bragg Liquid Aminos (see Shopping Guidelines)
- 3-4 boneless skinless chicken breasts, trimmed of fat and cut into 1 inch cubes
- 1 large onion, chopped
- 1 bag frozen vegetable stir fry OR
- 2 cups broccoli flowerets
- 1 cup chopped celery
- 1 cup chopped carrots
- ½ cup low sodium chicken broth
- 1 tablespoon Bragg Liquid Aminos
- 1 dash of ginger

Combine the first 3 ingredients in a plastic bag. Add chicken and shake to coat. Marinade in refrigerator 30 minutes.

Coat a large nonstick skillet with no fat/no calorie cooking spray. Heat to medium-high and add chicken and onion. Sauté 6-7 minutes or until chicken is cooked through and no longer pink. Remove chicken from skillet and keep warm.

Add bag of frozen vegetables, or freshly chopped vegetables, to the hot skillet. Sauté for 3 minutes stirring very frequently to prevent sticking. Add broth, 1 tablespoon of Bragg Liquid Aminos and a dash of ginger. Sauté about 1-2 more minutes or until liquid is mostly absorbed.

- *Sea Salt to taste*
- *¼ teaspoon black pepper*
- *¼ teaspoon dried thyme*
- *4 boneless skinless chicken breasts, trimmed of fat (best if pounded thin)*
- *½ cup (or one small) onion, chopped*
- *2 teaspoons minced garlic*
- *¾ cup dried mixed fruit (No Sugar Added, you have to be careful with this! Use raisins if you can't find dried mixed fruit without sugar in the ingredients list)*
- *1 cup low sodium chicken broth*
- *1 to 1 ½ tablespoon very finely diced potted green olives (No Sugar Added)*
- *⅛ teaspoon black pepper*

Spray a nonstick skillet with no fat/no calorie cooking spray. Heat over medium-high heat. Sprinkle chicken with sea salt to taste, ¼ teaspoon pepper, and thyme. Add to skillet and cook on each side until lightly browned and cooked through. (You may add coconut oil in very small amounts (1-2 teaspoon) if the chicken starts to burn or stick. ) Remove from skillet and keep warm.

In the same skillet, sauté onion for 2 minutes or until tender. Add garlic and sauté about 30 seconds. Add fruit and remaining ingredients to pan. Cook 5 minutes or until liquid almost evaporates. Pour over chicken.

*Can be served with 100% Whole Wheat Couscous

- o  *4 skinless boneless chicken breasts, trimmed of fat*
- o  *1 cup applesauce (No Sugar Added)*
- o  *½ cup water*
- o  *small onion, sliced*
- o  *1 tablespoon minced garlic*
- o  *2 teaspoons apple cider or white vinegar*
- o  *pinch of cinnamon*
- o  *½ teaspoon black pepper*
- o  *pinch of red pepper flakes (optional)*

Sauté the onion and garlic over medium-high heat in a non-stick skillet lightly coated with no fat/no calorie cooking spray. Add the chicken and sauté on both sides until browned. Add the rest of the ingredients and heat until bubbly. Reduce heat to medium-low, then cover and cook for 15 minutes or until the center is no longer pink.

*Can be converted to a slow cooker recipe by placing all ingredients in a slow cooker. Cover and cook for 3-4 hours on high or 6-7 hours on low.

- o  *3-4 boneless skinless chicken breasts, trimmed of fat*
- o  *½ cup chicken broth*
- o  *1 cup salsa (No Sugar Added)*
- o  *1 can low sodium black beans (rinsed and drained)*
- o  *2 cloves minced garlic*
- o  *1 teaspoon cumin*

Place chicken in slow cooker. Top with remaining ingredients. Cover and cook over low for 6-7 hours.

This can be served several ways. You can shred the chicken in the slow cooker, stir and serve. Or, you can remove the chicken breasts and top with the salsa mixture in the slow cooker. You can also have the leftover shredded mixture on a whole wheat tortilla or over lettuce for a Tex/Mex salad.

- o   3 boneless skinless chicken breasts, trimmed of fat
- o   1 medium onion, chopped
- o   1 green bell pepper, sliced
- o   1 jalapeño seeded and chopped
- o   2 cloves minced garlic
- o   1 T BSP freshly chopped cilantro
- o   1 teaspoon. chili powder
- o   1 teaspoon cumin
- o   1 teaspoon coriander
- o   ¾ teaspoon sea salt (optional)
- o   1 (10 oz..) can diced tomatoes with green chili peppers (Rotel)

Place all ingredients in slow cooker.  Cover and cook on high for 4-5 hours or low for hours.  Shred with a fork.

Serve over brown rice, wrap in a whole wheat tortilla, or create a lettuce wrap by wrapping in a large lettuce leaf.

- *3-4 boneless skinless chicken breasts, trimmed of fat*
- *1 (8 oz.) can tomato sauce (No Sugar Added)*
- *½ cup salsa*
- *1 package Low Sodium Taco Seasoning or 3 -4 tablespoon Homemade Taco Seasoning*
- *1 teaspoon chili powder*
- *1 teaspoon cumin*
- *2 cloves minced garlic*

Place chicken in slow cooker. Pour remaining ingredients on top of chicken. Cover and cook on low for 6 hours or until chicken is cooked through.

Serve over lettuce for a Tex-Mex inspired salad using the extra juice as a dressing or creating your own using some olive oil, lemon/lime juice, and taco seasoning.

Burrito or Salad Topping Suggestions: Black Beans (rinsed and drained), tomatoes, lettuce, black olives, salsa, avocado (make an avocado spread by mashing the avocado with some lemon juice)

# Chicken and Spinach Skillet Dish

- o  *1 to 2 stalks celery, chopped*
- o  *1 onion, diced*
- o  *3 – 4 thinly pounded chicken breasts*
- o  *½ of a fresh lemon*
- o  *¼ teaspoon garlic powder (or to taste)*
- o  *¼ teaspoon lemon pepper seasoning (or to taste)*
- o  *¾ to 1 cup chicken broth*
- o  *3 – 4 large handfuls fresh baby spinach*
- o  *⅛ cup of slivered almonds*

Lightly spray a large, nonstick skillet with no fat/no calorie cooking spray. Lightly sauté celery and onion about 1 -2 minutes, add chicken breasts and cook until almost cooked through on each side. Season with a very small amount of sea salt, pepper, garlic powder, and lemon pepper seasoning.

Squeeze lemons juice on top of chicken as it's cooking. Add almonds. Once chicken is almost finished add spinach (3-4 large handfuls or ½ bag- they shrink significantly). Pour broth over spinach. Cover and cook till chicken is done and spinach is cooked.

- o  2 tablespoons chicken broth
- o  6 skinless, boneless chicken breast halves , trimmed of fat
- o  3 cloves garlic, minced
- o  ½ cup diced onion
- o  3 cups tomatoes, chopped
- o  ½ cup chicken broth
- o  2 teaspoons chopped fresh thyme
- o  1 tablespoon chopped fresh basil
- o  ½ cup kalamata olives
- o  ¼ cup chopped fresh parsley
- o  salt and pepper to taste

Heat large non-stick skillet over medium heat and spray lightly with no fat/no calorie cooking spray.

Brown chicken 4-6 minutes on each side, until golden. Remove chicken from skillet and set aside. Sauté onion in pan drippings for 3 minutes, then add garlic and sauté for about 30 more seconds. Add tomatoes and bring to a boil. Lower heat and add remaining broth, thyme, and basil. Simmer for 5 minutes. Return chicken to the skillet and cover. Cook over low heat until the chicken is cooked through and no longer pink. Add olives and parsley to the skillet and cook for 1 minute. Season with salt and pepper to taste.

- o *1 pound skinless, boneless chicken breast trimmed of fat and cubed*
- o *Sea salt to taste*
- o *1 onion, chopped*
- o *2 cloves garlic, chopped*
- o *2 carrots, sliced*
- o *2 stalks celery, sliced*
- o *1 tablespoon minced fresh ginger root*
- o *½ teaspoon paprika*
- o *¾ teaspoon ground cumin*
- o *½ teaspoon dried oregano*
- o *¼ teaspoon ground cayenne pepper*
- o *¼ teaspoon ground turmeric*
- o *1 ½ cups chicken broth*
- o *1 cup crushed tomatoes*
- o *1 cup chickpeas, optional (frozen or if using canned look for low sodium variety)*
- o *1 zucchini, sliced*
- o *1 tablespoon lemon juice*

Season chicken with salt and brown in a large non-stick saucepan over medium heat until almost cooked through. Remove chicken from pan and set aside.

Sauté onion, garlic, carrots and celery in same pan. When tender, stir in ginger, paprika, cumin, oregano, cayenne pepper and turmeric; stir fry for about 1 minute, then mix in broth and tomatoes.

Return chicken to pan, reduce heat to low and simmer for about 10 minutes.

Add chickpeas and zucchini to pan and bring to simmering once again; cover pan and cook for about 15 minutes, or until zucchini is cooked through and tender. Stir in lemon juice and serve.

# Winter Chicken Bake

- 3 boneless skinless chicken breasts trimmed of fat
- 1 sweet potato
- ½ medium sweet onion, chopped
- 1 medium apple - peeled, cored, and chopped
- 3 carrots, peeled and chopped
- 2 tablespoons. Sugar Free BBQ Sauce (ex: Walden's Farms)
- 1 cup cranberries

Preheat oven to 375 degrees. Lightly grease a baking dish with no fat/no calorie cooking spray. Pierce the sweet potato several times with a fork and cut in half. Place in a microwave-safe dish; pour water to about ½-inch deep. Cook in microwave 10 minutes.

Arrange the onion, apple, and carrots into the bottom of the prepared baking dish. Brush the barbecue sauce on both sides of the chicken breasts and lay atop the vegetables. Peel the sweet potato and cut into large chunks; scatter into the baking dish. Sprinkle the cranberries over the dish. Bake in the preheated oven until the chicken is tender and no longer pink in the center, 45 to 55 minutes. Allow to cool 5 minutes before serving.

- ○ ½ teaspoon Tabasco sauce
- ○ ½ teaspoon ground pepper
- ○ 4 tablespoons white vinegar
- ○ 1 cup diced white onion
- ○ 2 cloves minced garlic
- ○ 1 (8 oz.) can tomato sauce
- ○ ½ teaspoon sea salt
- ○ 1 (15 oz.) can diced tomatoes (No Sugar Added, a "seasoned" variety is good if you can find one)
- ○ ½ teaspoon Worcestershire sauce
- ○ ½ teaspoon prepared mustard
- ○ ½ teaspoon paprika
- ○ 3-4 chicken breasts

Mix everything together (can be in a slow cooker or in a pot on the stove) then add the chicken. Stovetop: Cook on medium heat until the chicken is tender (at least an hour). Slow cooker: Cover and cook on high 3-4 hours, or low for 6-7 hours. Serve over brown rice.

- o  *1 pound Ground Turkey, Bison, or very lean Ground Beef*
- o  *100% Whole Wheat Spaghetti Noodles (preferably stone ground)*
- o  *1 large jar No Sugar Added Spaghetti Sauce*
- o  *2 cloves minced garlic*
- o  *1 medium onion, chopped*

In a large nonstick skillet brown meat with onion and garlic until meat is cooked through. Add jarred spaghetti sauce and simmer until heated through. Meanwhile, bring a large pot of water (unsalted!) to a boil and boil noodles according to package directions.

Tips for serving: It is best not to mix your noodles and meat mixture together so that you can control the amount of pasta and meat you consume. Using the appropriate portion size for your weight measure out your noodles and then meat.

- o   *1 pound Ground Turkey, Bison, or very lean Ground Beef*
- o   *100% Whole Wheat Pasta (whatever shape you'd like-preferably stone ground)*
- o   *1 large jar No Sugar Added Spaghetti Sauce*
- o   *2 cloves minced garlic*
- o   *1 medium onion, chopped*
- o   *1 medium bell pepper , chopped(green, red, or yellow or a combination of each)*
- o   *1 small box frozen chopped spinach*
- o   *1 (8 oz.) can tomato sauce (No Sugar Added)*
- o   *2 tablespoons fresh parsley, chopped*

Cook frozen chopped spinach according to package directions. Cool, drain, and squeeze as much of the excess liquid from the spinach as possible.  Spray a large nonstick skillet with no calorie/no fat cooking spray and brown meat with onions, garlic, and bell pepper until meat is cooked through.  Add spaghetti sauce, spinach, tomato sauce, and fresh parsley to the cooked meat. Simmer until heated through.

Meanwhile boil pasta according to package directions .

Tips for serving:  It is best not to mix your noodles and meat mixture together so that you can control the amount of pasta and meat you consume. Using the appropriate portion size for your weight measure out your pasta and meat and then mix the two together on your plate.

- o  *1 can low sodium, white meat tuna (in water), rinsed and drained*
- o  *1-2 tablespoons finely diced celery*
- o  *1-2 teaspoon sunflower seeds*
- o  *1 hard boiled egg, diced*
- o  *1-2 tablespoons Olive Oil Mayonnaise*

Mix all ingredients together, adding mayonnaise a little at a time until you reach your desired consistency. Can be eaten alone or served on 1 slice of 100% whole wheat bread, whole wheat tortilla, on a lettuce leaf wrap, or over a green salad.

## Zesty Tuna

- o  *1 can low sodium, white meat tuna (in water), rinsed and drained*
- o  *½ an avocado*
- o  *Freshly squeezed lemon juice to taste*
- o  *Pepper*
- o  *Freshly torn basil leaves*

Mix all ingredients as desired. Eat as is, or serve on 1 slice of 100% Whole Wheat Bread, or serve over a salad.

- 1 small bag dry red beans
- 1 small bag dry light kidney beans
- 1 pound ground turkey, bison or super lean ground beef
- 2 cloves minced garlic
- 1 large green bell pepper, diced
- 1 medium to large onion, diced
- 1 (29 oz.) can crushed tomato (No Sugar Added)
- 1 (15 oz.) can tomato sauce (No Sugar Added)
- ¼ cup (approx.) Chili Powder (more or less to desired taste)
- 2 teaspoons (approx.) cumin (to taste)

Prepare beans ahead of time according to package directions OR if you choose to use canned beans read the labels and look for a low sodium variety with no added sugar. It is best to prepare the beans yourself because the sodium content of canned beans is often quite high.

Brown meat, bell pepper, garlic, and onion in a large stock pot seasoning with black pepper as you brown. Add in all tomatoes. Drain beans and add a little at a time until desired consistency/amount. Season with chili powder and cumin until desired taste.

Simmer on low heat for about 30 minutes.

# Tex/Mex Chili

- 1 pound ground turkey, bison, or super lean ground beef
- 2 small cans of low sodium black beans, rinsed and drained
- 2 cloves minced garlic
- 1 medium green bell pepper, chopped
- 1 medium to large onion, chopped
- 1 (29 oz.) can crushed tomato (No Sugar Added)
- 1 (16oz) jar salsa (No Sugar Added)
- ¼ cup (approx.) Chili Powder (more or less to taste)
- 2 teaspoons (approx.) cumin (to taste)

Brown meat in a large stock pot along with garlic, bell pepper, and onion.

Add beans, tomatoes, salsa, and spices to taste.

Simmer on low heat for about 30 minutes.

# Meatloaf

- 1 – 1.5 pound 99% Fat Free Turkey Breast
- 1 egg OR 2 egg whites
- ½ cup tomato sauce (No Sugar Added)
- ¼ cup shredded carrots
- ½ cup chopped red/white onion
- ½ cup Old Fashioned Oats (not the quick cooking kind)
- ½ cup chopped bell pepper (any color green, yellow, orange or red)
- Dash of garlic powder
- Dash of basil
- Dash of Spike (salt free)

Mix all ingredients together, except for tomato sauce. Lightly grease a loaf pan with no fat/no calorie cooking spray. Place meat mixture in the loaf pan and top with tomato sauce.

Bake at 350 degrees for 1 hour.

- 3-4 boneless skinless chicken breasts, trimmed of fat
- 5 cloves chopped garlic
- 1 small onion, finely chopped
- ¼ cup Bragg Liquid Aminos (see Shopping Guidelines)
- ¼ cup low sodium chicken broth
- ½ teaspoon ground ginger
- 1 dash allspice (or a dash each of ground cloves, cinnamon, and black pepper)
- 2 tablespoons apple cider vinegar
- Optional: 1 small can of crushed pineapple

Bean sprouts and large leafy lettuce for wrapping

Place chicken in a slow cooker. Add onions and garlic. Mix the liquid and spices together and pour over chicken.

Cook on low about 4 hours.

Shred chicken in slow cooker and serve on lettuce with bean sprouts.

# Zesty Chicken Marinade

- o  *3 tablespoons Bragg Liquid Aminos (see Shopping Guidelines)*
- o  *2 tablespoons Worcestershire sauce (Sugar Free)*
- o  *2 tablespoons Red Wine Vinegar*
- o  *1 tablespoon Lemon Juice*
- o  *1 ½ teaspoon dry ground mustard*
- o  *¾ teaspoon black pepper*
- o  *1 teaspoon fresh parsley, minced*
- o  *2 tablespoons low sodium chicken broth*

Mix all ingredients in a plastic bag, seal and shake.

Add chicken and marinade at least 30 minutes or up to overnight.

Grill.

# Grilled Cajun Chicken

- 1 tablespoon Cajun seasoning
- 1 tablespoon dried Italian-style seasoning
- 1 tablespoon lemon pepper seasoning
- 1 dash of garlic powder

In a small container mix the spices together.

Rub into chicken breasts, cover and refrigerate until ready to grill.

- o *4 boneless skinless chicken breasts, trimmed of fat*
- o *½ cup lemon juice*
- o *½ teaspoon onion powder*
- o *Ground black pepper to taste*
- o *Seasoning salt to taste (look for a low sodium variety)*
- o *2 teaspoons dried parsley, cilantro, or oregano (whatever you have on hand or prefer)*

Dip chicken in lemon juice and arrange in a large baking dish. Sprinkle chicken breasts with seasonings and discard any remaining lemon juice.

Grill.

# Grilled Lemon Chicken

- ⅓ cup lemon juice
- ¼ cup chicken broth
- 1 tablespoon Dijon mustard
- 2 cloves minced garlic
- 2 tablespoons finely chopped red bell pepper
- ¼ teaspoon sea salt
- ¼ teaspoon black pepper
- 4 boneless skinless chicken breasts, trimmed of fat

In a plastic bag mix all ingredients together and shake well to coat chicken.

Marinade in refrigerator for at least 30 minutes and up to overnight.

Grill.

- ½ cup freshly squeezed juice from one orange (Avoid store bought orange juice)
- 2 teaspoons orange zest
- 2 tablespoons fresh lime juice
- 1 tablespoon balsamic vinegar
- 2 teaspoons minced fresh ginger root
- 3 cloves garlic, minced
- ¼ teaspoon hot pepper sauce
- 1 teaspoon chopped fresh oregano
- 3 - 4 boneless skinless chicken breasts

Mix all ingredients except chicken in a blender. Pour into a plastic bag. Add chicken. Seal, shake to coat, and marinade in refrigerator for 1 hour.

Grill.

*Serve with sweet potatoes.

# Zesty Bun-less Burgers

- 1 to 1.5 pounds very lean ground turkey, bison, or beef
- 1 tablespoon very finely minced onion
- 2 cloves minced garlic
- 1 cup salsa

Mix the raw ground meat, onion, and garlic in a bowl. Cover and marinade in refrigerator for 30 minutes. Form meat into patties and grill.

To serve, top each burger with salsa.

# Bun-less Burgers

- o *1 to 1.5 pounds very lean ground turkey, bison, or beef*
- o *1 tablespoon very finely minced onion*
- o *2 cloves minced garlic*
- o *Heinz Reduced Sugar Ketchup*
- o *Mustard*
- o *Chopped lettuce*
- o *Sliced tomato*

Mix the raw ground meat, onion, and garlic in a bowl. Cover and marinade in refrigerator for 30 minutes. Form meat into patties and grill.

To serve, top each burger with ketchup, mustard, lettuce and tomato.

- 1 to 1.5 pounds ground turkey, bison, or very lean beef
- 1 tablespoon very finely minced onion
- 2 cloves minced garlic
- 1 tablespoon Bragg Liquid Aminos (see Shopping Guidelines)
- 1 can pineapple slices (No Sugar Added, in their own juice)
- 1 green bell pepper cut into strips
- 1 large sweet onion, cut into strips

Mix the raw meat, onions, garlic, and Liquid Aminos in a bowl. Cover and marinade in refrigerator for 30minutes. Form meat into patties and grill until cooked through.

Grill sliced pineapple with the meat until heated through and tender. Meanwhile, in a large nonstick skillet, sauté onion and bell pepper until very tender.

To serve, top burger with a pineapple ring and sautéed vegetables.

- o  *1 pound extra lean ground beef, turkey, or bison*
- o  *1 onion, chopped*
- o  *1 bell pepper, chopped*
- o  *2 cloves minced garlic*
- o  *1 tablespoon lemon juice*
- o  *1 tablespoon mustard, prepared*
- o  *1 teaspoon chili powder*
- o  *2 tablespoons Bragg Liquid Aminos*
- o  *Dash cayenne pepper*
- o  *1 cup tomato sauce (No Sugar Added)*
- o  *1 can low sodium black beans, rinsed and drained*

Brown beef with onion, peppers, and garlic in a large nonstick skillet.

In a small bowl combine lemon juice, mustard, chili powder, Bragg Liquid Aminos, and cayenne with a small amount of tomato sauce and whisk until thoroughly blended.

Stir in remaining tomato sauce, then add to meat mixture. Add beans and cook for 20 minutes, or until flavors are well blended.

Serve over brown rice.

## Baked Tilapia

- o  *3 ounce tilapia filets*
- o  *olive oil*
- o  *salt*
- o  *pepper*
- o  *garlic powder*
- o  *dried minced garlic*

Preheat oven to 450°.

Coat glass baking dish with olive oil. Lightly coat the top of filets with olive oil. Season well with salt, pepper, garlic powder and lots of dried minced garlic.

Bake for 14 minutes, and then flip filets, coat and season the other side then bake for another 14 minutes.

Serve with steamed veggies.

# BBQ Chicken

- o *3-4 boneless skinless chicken breasts, trimmed of fat*
- o *¼ cup Sugar Free BBQ Sauce (ex:  Walden's Farms)*

Heat Grill.  Cook chicken on grill and baste frequently with BBQ sauce.

- o   2 cups brown rice
- o   4 cups water
- o   1.5 pounds very lean ground beef, turkey, or bison
- o   2 tablespoons Cajun seasoning
- o   1 onion, chopped
- o   2 (15oz) can black beans, rinsed and drained
- o   1 (6oz) can chopped black olives, rinsed and drained (optional)
- o   ¼ cup red wine vinegar
- o   3 sprigs fresh cilantro, chopped (optional)
- o   ¼ teaspoon chipotle powder (optional)

Place rice and water in a saucepan over medium heat. Bring to a boil, then reduce heat to a low and simmer for about 45 minutes, or until rice is tender.

While rice is cooking, brown the meat and onion in a deep nonstick skillet. Season with Cajun seasoning. Stir in beans, olives, vinegar, and chipotle powder.

Mix well, cover and simmer for 20 minutes over medium-low heat. Add the cilantro during the last 5 minutes of cooking.

Serve over rice.

- 1 tablespoon olive oil
- 4 cloves garlic, minced
- 1 (14-ounce) can low-sodium diced tomatoes, juice included
- 1 (12-ounce) can low-sodium tomato sauce
- 1 (7-ounce) jar roasted red peppers, drained, rinsed and thinly sliced
- 2 dried whole red chile peppers
- 1 teaspoon ground cumin
- ½ teaspoon ground coriander
- ½ teaspoon salt
- ½ teaspoon ground black pepper
- 1 large bunch Swiss chard, washed well and dried, tough center stems removed, coarsely
- chopped (about 8 cups)
- 4 (6-ounce) skinless salmon fillets
- ¼ cup chopped cilantro leaves

Preheat oven to 350 degrees F.

Heat oil in a large saute pan over medium-low heat. Add garlic and cook until soft and golden, about 1 minute. Add diced tomatoes with juice, tomato sauce, red peppers, chili peppers, cumin, coriander and ¼ teaspoon each salt and pepper.

Bring to a boil, then reduce heat to medium-low and simmer for 10 minutes until sauce thickens slightly. Remove from heat, and remove chile peppers.

Place Swiss chard on the bottom of a 9 by 13-inch glass baking dish. Season fish fillets with remaining salt and pepper and place in on top of chard.

Cover with sauce and bake, covered, until fish is just cooked and chard is wilted, about 15 minutes.

Remove cover and bake an additional 5 minutes. Sprinkle with cilantro and serve.

- 8 ounces 93%-lean ground beef
- 8 ounces 99%-lean ground turkey breast
- ½ cup chopped onion
- 1 10-ounce can diced tomatoes with green chilies, preferably Rotel brand (see Tip), or 1 ¼ cups
- petite-diced tomatoes
- ½ teaspoon ground cumin
- ½ teaspoon ground chipotle chile or 1 teaspoon chili powder
- ½ teaspoon dried oregano

Place beef, turkey and onion in a large nonstick skillet over medium heat. Cook, breaking up the meat with a wooden spoon, until cooked through, about 10 minutes.

Transfer to a colander to drain off fat. Wipe out the pan.

Return the meat to the pan and add tomatoes, cumin, ground chipotle (or chili powder) and oregano. Cook over medium heat, stirring occasionally, until most of the liquid has evaporated, 3 to 6 minutes.

Look for Rotel brand diced tomatoes with green chilies - original or mild, depending on your spice preference - and set the heat level with either ground chipotle chile (adds smoky heat) or chili powder (adds rich chili taste without extra spice).

Eat alone, on a Whole Wheat Tortilla, or over a salad.

# Grilled Basil-Marinated Chicken

- o  1 tablespoon olive oil
- o  1 tablespoon red wine vinegar
- o  1 tablespoon chopped basil leaves, plus 4 sprigs for garnish
- o  1 tablespoon finely chopped red onion
- o  2 teaspoons kosher salt
- o  1 teaspoon whole black peppercorns
- o  1 clove garlic, chopped
- o  4 boneless, skinless chicken breast halves (about 2 pounds)

Whisk together the oil, vinegar, basil, onion, salt, peppercorns, and garlic in a bowl. Transfer the marinade to a gallon-sized sealable plastic bag with the chicken and shake to combine. Refrigerate for at least 3 hours and up to 12 hours.

Remove chicken from the marinade. Grill the chicken, turning once, until browned and just cooked through, about 4 minutes per side. Transfer the chicken to a platter and garnish with the basil sprigs.

- 1 small bag baby spinach leaves
- 1-2 pounds salmon filets
- 1 lemon, sliced
- Dill to taste
- Salt and pepper to taste
- ¼ cup chicken broth.

Fill slow cooker with spinach leaves. Top with salmon filets and sprinkle with salt, pepper, and dill to taste. Top with lemon slices and pour chicken broth over the top.

Cover and cook on low for 2 hours. Salmon should flake and be fully cooked.

# Country Captain Slow Cooker Chicken

- 1 ¾ pounds boneless, skinless chicken breast (frozen is fine)
- 2 Granny Smith apples, peeled, cored, and diced
- 1 onion, peeled and diced
- 1 green bell pepper, seeded and diced
- 3 cloves garlic, minced
- 1 tablespoon curry powder
- 1 teaspoon ground ginger
- ½ teaspoon kosher salt
- ¼ teaspoon cayenne pepper
- ¼ cup raisins
- 1 (14.5-ounce) can diced tomatoes
- ½ cup chicken broth
- 1 cup raw long-grain basmati brown rice (to add later)

Use a 6-quart slow cooker. Put the chicken into the bottom of your stoneware. Add chopped apple, onion, and bell pepper. Add garlic and all spices. Toss in the raisins and the entire can of diced tomatoes. Stir in the chicken broth.

Cover and cook on low for 6 hours, or until chicken is tender, but still intact.

Using tongs, remove chicken carefully from the slow cooker and place in a covered dish to keep warm. Stir in raw brown rice. Cover and cook again for about 30-40 minutes, or until rice is bite-tender.

Serve rice on a plate with chicken pieces arranged on top.

# Marmalade Curry Chicken

- 4 boneless, skinless chicken breast halves or thighs
- 1 (18-ounce) jar orange marmalade (sugar-free)
- 1 ½ teaspoons curry powder
- ½ teaspoon cayenne pepper (Or to your spice preference)
- ¼ teaspoon ground ginger
- ¼ teaspoon kosher salt
- ¼ cup chicken broth

Use a 4 quart slow cooker. Put the chicken into the bottom of your slow cooker. In a small bowl, combine the marmalade with the dry spices and chicken broth. Pour this on top of the chicken.

Cover and cook on low for 6 to 7 hours, or on high for about 4.

If when fully cooked the chicken isn't quite as moist as you'd like, you can cut it into strips, then return it to the pot to soak in even more of the yummy sauce.

Serve over brown basmati rice.

- 1 pound of turkey breast cutlets
- 1 can tomatoes and chilies
- 2 mangoes
- 2 peaches
- 1 T dried minced onion
- ¼ cup water
- Cilantro (optional)

Peel and chop up the fruit. In a small bowl, combine the can of tomatoes and chilies with the chopped fruit, water, and dried onion flakes. (and optional cilantro)

Lay the pieces of meat into the bottom of the slow cooker-- slightly stagger the pieces so they don't stick together. Cover with your newly-made salsa.

Cook on low for 5-8 hours, or on high for 3-4. If you use turkey, it will be a bit tough if you cook it on high.

# Warm Pineapple and Chicken Salad

- o *3 boneless skinless chicken breast halves*
- o *20 oz. can of pineapple chunks*
- o *¼ cup Bragg Liquid Aminos*
- o *1 teaspoon red pepper flakes*
- o *1 bag baby spinach leaves*
- o *1 tablespoon red onion, finely sliced*
- o *1-2 tablespoons slivered almonds (lightly browned in oven)*

Place chicken in slow cooker. Drain pineapple, reserving juice. Pour Bragg Liquid Aminos, pineapple chunks, and ¼ cup pineapple juice (from the can) over the chicken. Sprinkle flakes on top.

Cover and cook on high 4 hours or low 6-7 hours.

Serve pineapple and chicken over the spinach leaves. Top with red onion and slivered almonds if desired.

# Slow Cooked Rice and Chicken

- ○ *Garlic, crushed*
- ○ *Bit of fresh ginger, minced*
- ○ *Celery, diced*
- ○ *Mushrooms*
- ○ *Brown rice*
- ○ *Chicken stock*
- ○ *Cooked chicken, shredded*
- ○ *Pepper*
- ○ *Sesame oil*
- ○ *Bragg Liquid Aminos*
- ○ *Green onions, chopped*

Put everything, except the cooked chicken into slow-cooker. Add ingredients based on your individual preferences.

Cook at high for about 4 hours, and then low for about 4-6 more hours.

Before serving, stir in the cooked, shredded chicken. When ready to serve, ladle desired amount into a bowl, drizzle in sesame oil and Bragg Liquid Aminos, and top with green onions.

- o 3-4 boneless skinless chicken breast halves, diced into 1 inch cubes
- o 1 teaspoon sea salt
- o Juice of 1 lime
- o 2 tablespoons coconut oil
- o 3 small onions, coarsely chopped
- o 3 garlic cloves, minced
- o 2 quarter sized pieces fresh ginger, peeled and minced
- o 1-2 tablespoons curry powder to taste
- o 3 large tomatoes, chopped, plus 1 cup tomato juice or 1 14oz can tomatoes plus juice
- o 1 ½ cups canned cubed pineapple plus ¼ cup juice

Sprinkle the chicken with the salt and lime juice, set aside. Heat the coconut oil in large skillet. Add the chicken and cook until brown on both sides and cooked through. Remove and set aside. Add the onions, garlic and ginger.

Cook over medium heat, stirring often, until the onions are translucent, about 5 minutes. Add the curry powder, stir well, and continue to sauté the mixture for 3 more minutes, stirring frequently. Add the tomatoes and juice, and pineapple juice.

Stir, cover, and let simmer for 15 minutes, stirring occasionally. Uncover the skillet and add the pineapple and and return the chicken to the skillet. Stir well and cook over medium heat for 3-5 minutes.

Can be served over brown rice.

- *2 pounds white fish (tuna or shark work well)*
- *2 mangoes, peeled and sliced*

Marinade :

- *1 tablespoon peeled and minced fresh ginger*
- *¼ cup fresh cilantro*
- *2 tablespoons Bragg Liquid Aminos (see Shopping Guidelines)*
- *¼ cup fresh lime juice*
- *1/3 cup olive oil*
- *1 tablespoon mustard*

Place all the marinade ingredients in a ziploc bag or container with a lid and shake well. Place the mangoes in a blender or food processor and puree to a coarse consistency; some tiny junks of mango should remain. Mix the mango puree with the marinade in a glass or ceramic dish just large enough to hold the fish. Place the fish in the marinade and turn several times to coat. Cover the fish with the marinade and place in refrigerator for 45 minutes. Do not marinate longer or the fish will begin to "cook" the acidic ingredients of the marinade.

Remove fish from marinade and place the marinade in a small saucepan. Gently warm over low heat. If sautéing the fish, add the fish along with the marinade to a large skillet and cook until done, about 10 minutes. Otherwise, grill fish (small, kebab-sized pieces of fish can also be marinated and grilled/sautéed), or put fish under broiler. Cook approximately 5 minutes on each side. Place fish on plates and spoon a bit of the warmed marinade over the fish and serve immediately with veggies or salad.

# Black Bean- Mango Salsa Wrap

- o   *4 whole wheat wraps*
- o   *1 (15oz) can, no added salt black beans*
- o   *3 tablespoon chunky salsa (no sugar added)*
- o   *½ teaspoon ground cumin*
- o   *1 medium, ripe mango, peeled and cubed*
- o   *¼ cup diced red onion*
- o   *½ cup diced avocado*
- o   *1 tablespoon chopped fresh cilantro*
- o   *1tsp olive oil*
- o   *1tsp lemon juice*

Mixed greens salad (lettuce, tomato, cucumber, etc)

Grilled Chicken (this is a great way to use up leftover grilled chicken)

In a medium bowl, mash black beans with fork until mushy and add salsa and cumin. Mix well. Store the bean mixture in an airtight container to use as a sandwich spread for the week.

To make the salsa, place the mango cubes, onion, and avocado in a bowl. In a separate bowl, whisk together olive oil and lemon juice. Pour over mango mixture. Stir well and store in air tight container as sandwich topper for week.

Make medium bowl of mixed greens salad: lettuce, tomato, cucumber etc. Store in air tight container for the week.

Wrap assembly: Take the tortilla, spread with roughly 1/3 of black bean mixture, sprinkle on ¼ cup mango salsa, and top with a hearty helping of salad mix and grilled chicken. Roll up and wrap with foil. Pack for lunch!

# Veggie Packed Sloppy Joe's

- 1 pound lean ground beef or turkey
- ½ cup mushrooms
- 3 celery sticks
- 4 cherry tomatoes
- ½ green bell pepper
- ½ red bell pepper
- ½ cup black olives
- 1 cup water
- Salt-free seasoning
- 1 cup of water
- 4 whole wheat rolls/bread

Chop and puree all veggies in food processor.

Brown the beef (turkey) and drain any fat. Add the water, seasoning, and pureed veggies to the meat.

Bring to a boil, and then let simmer for 10 minutes.

Serve on ½ of a whole wheat hamburger roll or 1 slice of bread.

- o  1 onion, chopped
- o  1 small head of garlic, chopped
- o  8 oz. mushrooms, chopped
- o  1 head broccoli, chopped
- o  2 red bell peppers, diced
- o  1 package firm tofu
- o  ½ teaspoon cayenne pepper (optional)
- o  1 teaspoon dried oregano
- o  1 teaspoon dried basil
- o  1 teaspoon dried rosemary
- o  2 jars marinara/spaghetti sauce (no sugar added)
- o  2 boxes whole wheat lasagna noodles, uncooked
- o  16 oz. frozen spinach, thawed and drained
- o  2 sweet potatoes, cooked and mashed
- o  6 roma tomatoes, thinly sliced
- o  1 cup raw cashews, ground

Preheat oven to 400F.

Sauté the onion and garlic on high heat for 3 minutes in a nonstick pan. Add the mushrooms and cook until the onions are limp and the mushrooms give up their liquid. Remove them to a large bowl. Reserve the mushroom liquid in a pan to sauté the other veggies.

Sauté the broccoli for 5 minutes and add to the mushroom bowl. Sauté the peppers until they just begin to soften. Add them to the veggie bowl.

Drain the tofu by wrapping in paper towels, and pressing. Break it up directly in the towel and stir it into the veggie bowl.

Add cayenne and herbs to the veggie bowl and stir.

To assemble, cover the bottom of a 9x13 inch casserole with a layer of sauce. Add a layer of noodles and cover the noodles with sauce. Spread the veggie mixture over the sauced noodles. Cover with a layer of noodles and another dressing of sauce. Top with the spinach. Cover the spinach with the mashed sweet potatoes. Add another layer of sauce, the final layer of noodles, and the last topping of sauce.

Cover the lasagna with thinly sliced tomatoes. Cover with foil and bake in oven for 45 minut4es. Remove foil, sprinkle with the cashews, and return to the oven for 15 minutes. Let sit 15 minutes before serving.

Makes 12 servings.

Be sure to consider your portion sizes (especially for protein and carbs). This dish leans more toward being a side dish with the carbs (sweet potatoes and noodles).

# Grilled Tuna Steak

- o *Tuna Steaks*
- o *Bragg Liquid Aminos (see Shopping Guidelines)*
- o *Minced garlic*
- o *Touch of olive oil*
- o *Touch of lemon juice*

Place steaks in a baking dish and sprinkle  with desired amount of soy sauce, garlic, olive oil, and lemon juice.

Cover and refrigerate for 30 minutes.

Grill for about 4 minutes on each side (for a medium-cooked tuna, depending on thickness)

- o  *1 pound lean turkey or extra lean ground beef*
- o  *2 tablespoons extra virgin olive oil*
- o  *1 large onion, minced*
- o  *1 cup prepared short-grain brown rice*
- o  *1 ¾ cups water*
- o  *6 medium red or green bell peppers*
- o  *½ cup pine nuts*
- o  *¼ cup fresh mint, minced*
- o  *¼ cup fresh parsley, minced*
- o  *¼ cup fresh lemon juice*
- o  *½ teaspoon ground cinnamon*

Heat olive oil in a saucepan and sauté onion and meat over medium heat until cooked through, about 10 minutes.

Meanwhile, bring a large pot of water to a boil. Cut off the tops of the peppers. Gently remove the cores and seeds to create an empty cavity. Blanch the peppers in the boiling water for 5 minutes. Remove from the water and place upside down on paper towels to drain.

Roast the pine nuts on a baking sheet in a preheated 350F oven for about 5 minutes. Remove and set aside, leaving the oven on for the peppers. In a large bowl mix together the browned meat with the rice, pine nuts, herbs, lemon juice, and cinnamon, salt, and pepper . Mix well and adjust the seasonings to taste. Stuff the peppers with the rice mixture, put the tops back on the peppers, and place them in a baking dish just large enough to hold them upright.

Bake for 25-30 minutes, or until heated through. Serve immediately.

- *2 cups lentils*
- *3 cups chicken broth*
- *3 cups water*
- *1 small yellow onion, diced*
- *1 cup diced celery*
- *1 teaspoon cumin*
- *½ teaspoon coriander*
- *1 teaspoon kosher salt*
- *½ teaspoon dried mustard*
- *½ teaspoon turmeric*
- *4 cloves garlic, chopped*
- *1 (4 ounce) can diced green chilies (hot or mild, your choice)--no need to drain (No Sugar Added)*
- *1 tablespoon dried parsley (or ¼ cup finely chopped fresh)*
- *3-4 large chicken breast halves*

Use a 4 to 5 quart slow cooker. Rinse the lentils under cold water until it runs clear. Dump into the slow cooker. Add broth and water. Add diced onion and celery. Add all spices, the garlic, and chilies. Stir to combine. Lay chicken breast halves on top of the assembled food.

Cover and cook on low for about 7 hours, or on high for about 4 hours. Before serving, remove chicken from the slow cooker, chop it up, and stir back in.

Serve over basmati rice if desired.

- o *Chicken tenderloins*
- o *2 Eggplants, peeled and sliced*
- o *2 Jars marinara/spaghetti sauce (No Sugar Added)*
- o *Capers (optional)*

Preheat oven to 350 F.

Spread some of the tomato sauce in bottom of baking dish. Add eggplant. Add layer of sauce.  Add layer of chicken. Add layer of sauce. Add layer of eggplants. Top of with layer of sauce. Sprinkle capers on top.

Bake uncovered for 30-40 minutes or until chicken is done

Can be eaten over brown rice.

- o *2 tablespoons olive oil*
- o *1 tablespoon lemon juice*
- o *½ teaspoon dried thyme leaves*
- o *¼ teaspoon mustard*
- o *Pinch of garlic powder*
- o *½ of a ripe avocado*
- o *2 cups chopped chicken (you can use canned, low sodium white meat chicken)*
- o *1 stalk celery, chopped*

Combine the first 5 ingredients in a salad bowl and whisk together with a fork until emulsified.

Slice avocado into small chunks and gently stir into dressing to coat. Stir in chicken and celery into avocado mixture and serve.

Enjoy on 1 slice of Whole Wheat Bread, in a Whole Wheat Tortilla, or over a bed of salad greens.

# Baked Tilapia with Dill Sauce

- 4 fillets of tilapia
- Salt and pepper to taste
- 1 tablespoon Cajun seasoning (or to taste)
- 1 lemon, thinly sliced
- ¼ cup Olive Oil Mayonnaise
- 1 dash garlic powder
- 1 teaspoon lemon juice
- 1 large sprig of fresh dill weed (or 1 teaspoon dried)

Preheat oven to 350 degrees. Lightly grease a 9x13 inch baking dish. Arrange tilapia on the baking dish and sprinkle evenly with salt, pepper, and Cajun seasoning. Top each fillet with 2-3 slices of lemon. Bake, uncovered, for 15-20 minutes or until the fish flakes easily with a fork.

Meanwhile mix the mayonnaise, garlic powder, lemon juice, and dill in a small bowl. Serve approximately 1 tablespoon with each fillet for dipping. Asparagus pairs nicely with this meal.

o *2 large red bell peppers, halved lengthwise with seeds and pith removed*
o *1 ½ cups chopped tomatoes (~ 3 Roma tomatoes)*
o *¾ cup fresh bruschetta sauce or marinara/spaghetti sauce (No Sugar Added)*
o *Ground turkey*

Preheat oven to 350F.

Place pepper halves on baking dish. Mix tomatoes, sauce and ground turkey in bowl. Stuff mixture inside pepper halves.

Place in oven and bake uncovered for 30-35 minutes.

Variation: Add pine nuts (or add cooked brown rice on refuel day/cleanse)

# Easy Tofu (Or Chicken) Stir Fry

- o ½ brick Organic Tofu (regular), cut into ½-inch cubes
- o 1 tablespoon extra-virgin olive oil
- o 1 teaspoon toasted sesame oil
- o 10 drops hot & spicy chili oil
- o 4 cups stir fry veggies (i.e. napa cabbage, broccoli florets, white cabbage, and/or bok choy)
- o Bragg Liquid Aminos

Heat a wok or wide saucepan on high and add all oils. Add tofu and stir-fry for 2 minutes. Reduec heat to medium-high, add veggies and soy sauce, and continue to stir-fry for an additional 3 minutes or until broccoli is bright green.

Variation: Use chicken instead of tofu and marinate in soy sauce for a few minutes.

- o  *2 tablespoons coconut oil*
- o  *1 onion, chopped*
- o  *2 stalks of celery, chopped*
- o  *4 oz. sliced mushroom*
- o  *Garlic powder to taste*
- o  *1/3 pound lean beef or ground turkey*
- o  *1 (28 oz.) can diced tomatoes*
- o  *2 tablespoons almond butter*
- o  *Cayenne pepper to taste*

In large pot over high heat, sauté chopped veggies in coconut oil and garlic powder until done. Add beef or turkey, stirring constantly until meat is cooked through. Add in canned tomatoes, cayenne pepper, and almond butter.

Turn heat to low, and allow the chili to simmer for about 10 minutes. Remove from heat. The chili will thicken the longer it cools.

# Sweet Potato Chili

- Sweet potatoes, peeled and in 2-inch chunks
- 1 yellow onion, diced
- 2 garlic cloves, minced
- 1 (15-oz) can red kidney beans, drained and rinsed (or ⅔ cup dried beans, soaked overnight and boiled briskly for 10 minutes)
- 1 red bell pepper, seeded and chopped
- 1 (14.5-oz) can tomatoes
- 1 tablespoon chili powder
- 1 teaspoon smoked paprika
- 1 teaspoon chipotle chili powder
- ½ teaspoon kosher salt
- 1 cup water
- ½ cup freshly squeezed juice from an orange (or water if you do not have an orange)

Use a 5-6 quart slow cooker. Peel and chunk the sweet potato and add to the pot. Add diced onion. Follow with the red bell pepper, can of tomatoes, the beans, garlic, and seasonings. Pour in juice from orange or water.

Cover and cook on low for 6-8 hours, or until the onion is translucent and the sweet potato is fork-tender (if you want the sweet potato to disappear when stirred, cook longer).

# Side Dishes

- o  *12 hard-boiled eggs*
- o  *¼ cup Olive Oil mayonnaise*
- o  *2 tablespoons vinegar*
- o  *½ teaspoon pepper*
- o  *¼ teaspoon salt*
- o  *½ cup frozen chopped spinach*

Cook spinach following package instructions and squeeze dry. Slice the eggs in half lengthwise; remove yolks and set whites aside.

In a small bowl, mash yolks with a fork. Gradually stir in the mayonnaise, vinegar, pepper and salt. Add spinach and mix well. Spoon into the egg whites.

# Ratatouille

- o  *2 small to medium zucchini's, 1 inch dice*
- o  *2 small to medium yellow squash, 1 inch dice*
- o  *1 medium onion, 1 inch dice*
- o  *1 (15 oz.) can diced OR stewed tomatoes (No Added Sugar!)*
- o  *Sea salt and pepper to taste*
- o  *1 handful of fresh flat leaf parsley, chopped*

Heat a skillet over medium high heat and lightly spray with no fat/no calorie cooking oil.  Add garlic, zucchini, squash, and onions.

Toss vigorously for 5-8 minutes, or until vegetables are tender.  Add tomatoes, salt, pepper, and parsley.  Reduce heat and simmer for 6 - 8 minutes or until thickened.

# Roasted Vegetables

- *2 cups zucchini (1 inch dice)*
- *2 cups yellow squash (1 inch dice)*
- *2 medium Vidalia/sweet onions (roughly chopped)*
- *1 cup cherry or Roma tomatoes (sliced)*
- *2 teaspoon coconut oil*
- *Sea salt and pepper (to taste)*

Place zucchini, squash, and onion in a large Ziploc bag. Add melted coconut oil and shake to coat vegetables. Place vegetables on a large jelly roll pan that has been lightly greased with no fat/ no calorie cooking spray. Sprinkle very lightly with sea salt and pepper to taste.

Bake at 450 degrees for 10-15 minutes watching carefully and stirring occasionally to prevent burning. Add tomatoes and cook for 5 more minutes or until tomatoes are starting to wilt and are heated through.

Serve immediately.

*You can experiment/add all kinds of other vegetables to this such as asparagus, carrots, etc.

# Tex-Mex Rice

- o  *1 cup dry brown rice (not the fast cooking kind)*
- o  *2 cloves minced garlic*
- o  *2 ¼ cups water or low sodium chicken broth*
- o  *1 cup salsa (No Sugar Added)*

In a large sauce pan sauté rice and garlic until lightly browned. Stir in water/broth and salsa.

Bring to a boil, reduce heat. Cover and simmer for approximately 30 minutes or until rice is tender and liquid is absorbed.

## Spanish Rice

- 1 ¼ cup chicken broth
- 1 cup tomato sauce
- 2 onions, diced
- 1 cup uncooked brown rice
- 2 tomatoes, diced
- 2 green bell peppers, diced
- ½ teaspoon chili powder
- Sea salt and pepper to taste
- 1 (10 oz) can sliced black olives, rinsed and drained (optional)

Spray a large nonstick pan with no fat/no calorie cooking spray. Heat and sauté onion and bell pepper until tender. Add uncooked rice to and sauté until lightly browned. Stir in chicken broth, tomato sauce, chili powder, tomatoes, salt and pepper to taste, and black olives (optional).

Bring to a boil. Cover, reduce heat and simmer for 30-35 minutes (or whatever time the package of brown rice suggests) until rice is tender and liquid is absorbed.

# Pineapple Brown Rice

- o  *1 large can pineapple tidbits (No Sugar Added, in its own juice)*
- o  *1 cup uncooked brown rice*
- o  *1 red bell pepper, chopped (optional)*
- o  *Sea salt and pepper to taste*

Strain pineapple juice into a large measuring cup. Add water to the juice to equal 2/14 cups of liquid.

In a large pot lightly sauté bell pepper for 2-3 minutes. Add rice , pineapple tidbits, and then pineapple juice/water mixture. Season with salt and pepper to taste.

Bring to a boil over high heat. Cover, reduce heat and simmer for 30 minutes or until rice is tender and liquid is absorbed.

- o  *4 sweet potatoes, cut into large French fries*
- o  *1 tablespoon water*
- o  *2 teaspoon Italian seasoning*
- o  *½ teaspoon lemon pepper seasoning*
- o  *1 pinch salt and pepper to taste*
- o  *2 teaspoon coconut oil*

Preheat oven to 400 degrees.

Place cut sweet potatoes into a microwave-safe dish with water. Cook in microwave for 5 minutes on full power. Drain off liquid and toss with Italian seasoning, lemon pepper, salt, pepper, and coconut oil.

Arrange fries in a single layer on a baking sheet. Bake for 30 minutes, turning once, or until fries are crispy on the outside.

- *1 cup 100% whole wheat couscous*
- *1 ½ cups boiling water*
- *1 clove garlic, minced*
- *¼ cup diced red bell pepper*
- *4 green onions, sliced*
- *1 cup cherry tomatoes*
- *1 cup fresh basil leaves*
- *1 pinch salt*
- *1 pinch ground black pepper*
- *1 dash balsamic vinegar*

Preheat oven to 350 degrees.

Stir couscous into boiling water and return water to a boil. Cover and remove pot from heat. Let stand 5 minutes, then fluff with a fork.

While couscous is cooking, heat a large nonstick skillet and spray with cooking spray. Sauté onions, peppers, and garlic over medium heat for 3 minutes. Stir in tomatoes, basil, cooked couscous, salt and pepper.

Mix together and transfer to a 1.5 quart casserole dish. Splash some balsamic vinegar on top.

Bake in a preheated 350 degree oven for 20 minutes.

- o   *2 to 2 ½ cups low sodium vegetable broth (depending on how dry you like your couscous)*
- o   *1/3 cup chopped dates*
- o   *1/3 cup chopped dried apricots (No Sugar Added)*
- o   *1/3 cup golden raisins*
- o   *2 cups dry 100% Whole Wheat couscous*
- o   *1 to 3 teaspoons ground cinnamon (as desired)*
- o   *½ cup slivered almonds, toasted*

Pour the vegetable broth into a large saucepan, and bring to a boil. Add the apricots, dates and raisins.

Boil for 2 to 3 minutes. Remove from the heat, and stir in the couscous. Cover, and let stand for 5 minutes. Stir in the cinnamon and toasted almonds, and serve.

*You can substitute the dried fruits for whatever is on sale, just check to make certain there are no added sugars!

# Couscous with Dried Fruit

- o  *1 cup chicken broth*
- o  *¼ cup water*
- o  *Sea salt to taste*
- o  *ground black pepper to taste*
- o  *1 cup uncooked 100% whole wheat couscous*

*¼ cup dried fruit (Read ingredients list to check for added sugar! Try any dried fruit such as sour cherries, golden raisins, dried cranberries, apricots, etc.)*

In a 2 quart saucepan, combine chicken broth, water, dried fruit, salt and pepper.

Cook over high heat until boiling. Stir in couscous, cover, and remove from heat. Let stand 5 minutes.

Fluff with a fork, and serve immediately.

- *2 tablespoons pine nuts*
- *1 ½ pounds asparagus*
- *1 large shallot, thinly sliced*
- *2 teaspoons extra-virgin olive oil*
- *¼ teaspoon salt, divided*
- *Freshly ground pepper to taste*
- *¼ cup balsamic vinegar*

Preheat oven to 350° F.

Spread pine nuts in a small baking pan and toast in the oven until golden and fragrant, 7 to 10 minutes. Transfer to a small bowl to cool.

Increase oven temperature to 450° F. Snap off the tough ends of asparagus. Toss the asparagus with shallot, oil, ⅛ teaspoon salt and pepper. Spread in a single layer on a large baking sheet with sides.

Roast, turning twice, until the asparagus is tender and browned, 10 to 15 minutes.

Meanwhile, bring vinegar and the remaining ⅛ teaspoon salt to a simmer in a small skillet over medium-high heat. Reduce heat to medium-low and simmer, swirling the pan occasionally, until slightly syrupy and reduced to 1 tablespoon, about 5 minutes. To serve, toss the asparagus with the reduced vinegar and sprinkle with the pine nuts.

# Quick Pasta-Veggie Medley

- o  *Water*
- o  *1 stalk broccoli, florets and stems*
- o  *1 zucchini*
- o  *8 oz. whole wheat pasta or udon noodles*
- o  *1 cup cooked chick-peas*
- o  *1 tablespoon extra-virgin olive oil*
- o  *1 medium tomato, diced*
- o  *Freshly ground pepper*

Bring a large pot of water to a boil. While water is coming to a boil prepare veggies. Cut broccoli (into florets and stems into thin matchsticks). Cut zucchini into similarly sized matchsticks. Set aside.

When water has come to a rolling boil, add pasta and cook according to package directions or until al-dente. Add the broccoli, zucchini and chickpeas. Cook for 1 minute. Drain pasta and veggies in a colander. Place in a large bowl and toss with the olive oil and tomatoes. Add pepper to taste.

Serve with Grilled Chicken.

# Barley with Kalamata Olives and Tomatoes

- o  3 cups water
- o  2 cups pearl barley
- o  1 ½ teaspoon sea salt
- o  ½ cup freshly squeezed lemon juice
- o  ¼ extra virgin olive oil
- o  1 tablespoon dried oregano
- o  1 pound tomatoes, seeded and cut into ½-inch pieces
- o  ¾ cup kalamata olives, pitted and quartered
- o  ¾ cup finely diced red onion
- o  ⅔cups finely chopped fresh Italian parsley
- o  ⅔ cup finely chopped green onions (white and green parts)
- o  3 tablespoons chopped fresh dill

Combine the water, barley, and salt in a large saucepan. Cover and bring to a boil over high heat.

Decrease the heat to medium-low and simmer about 40 minutes, until tender. Transfer to a large bowl. If you're serving this dish as a cold salad, refrigerate the barley while preparing the remaining ingredients.

Whisk the lemon juice, olive oil, and oregano in a bowl to blend. Pour the vinaigrette over the barley and toss to coat. Add the tomatoes, olives, red onion, parsley, green onions, and dill and toss again to combine. Season to taste with salt and pepper and serve cold or at room temperature.

The salad will keep for 2 days, covered and refrigerated. Toss again before serving.

# Peanut Noodle Salad

- o  *8 oz. whole wheat spaghetti*
- o  *1 tablespoon olive oil*
- o  *1 large stalk celery, peeled and finely chopped*
- o  *3 scallions (white and green parts), chopped on an angle*
- o  *For the dressing:*
- o  *1 tablespoon olive oil*
- o  *1 garlic clove*
- o  *¼ cup creamy peanut butter (no sugar added)*
- o  *1tablespoon stevia (optional)*
- o  *Juice of 1 lime*
- o  *¼ cup water*

Bring a large pot of water to a boil. Salt the water and add the noodles. Cook according to package directions, but drain 1-2 minutes shy of suggested cooking time to achieve "al dente" texture. Drain noodles well and rinse thoroughly with cold water.

While noodles cook, heat 1 tablespoon olive oil in a skillet over medium-low. Add celery and cook 2 minutes. Add scallions and cook 1-2 minutes. Remove from heat and transfer to a mixing bowl. Add the cooked noodles.

Make the dressing: Combine all dressing ingredients in a blender. Blend until creamy and very smooth. Pour dressing over noodles and veggies. Toss to coat.

Chill salad in fridge for at least 1 hour before serving. Just before serving, toss the salad thoroughly.

# Veggie Quinoa Salad

- o   1 tablespoon olive oil
- o   3 cloves garlic, crushed
- o   1 cup dry quinoa
- o   2 cups water (or vegetable broth)
- o   1 teaspoon chicken seasoning (salt free or low sodium)
- o   1 red onion
- o   1 red bell pepper
- o   1 cucumber
- o   2 Roma tomatoes
- o   Dressing:
- o   Juice of 1 lime
- o   3 tablespoon olive oil
- o   ¼ teaspoon ground cumin
- o   1 tablespoon chopped fresh cilantro
- o   1 tablespoon chopped fresh parsley
- o   1 teaspoon salt

Add the 1 tablespoon of olive oil, garlic and dried quinoa to a non-stick skillet. Allow to brown on medium-high heat for about 2-5 minutes. Add water and chicken seasoning and turn to high.

Once it boils, turn heat down and cover. Allow to cook about 15 minutes. Once the quinoa is cooked, remove from heat and allow to cool.

Meanwhile, chop up the veggies and set aside. The veggies are good when cut small (size of a kernel of corn). Mix up the dressing and set aside.

Once quinoa is cool, toss all together and serve.

# Miscellaneous

- ○ *2 heads garlic*
- ○ *½ cups reduced-sodium chicken broth*
- ○ *¼ cup wine or cider vinegar*
- ○ *2 tablespoons extra-virgin olive oil*
- ○ *2 teaspoons Dijon mustard*
- ○ *Salt & freshly ground pepper to taste*

Preheat oven to 400°F.

Pull off excess papery outside skin from garlic without separating the cloves. Slice ½ inch off the top of each head. Wrap individually in aluminum foil. Roast for 40 minutes, or until the garlic is very soft.

Unwrap the garlic and cool slightly. Separate the cloves and peel. Combine garlic cloves, broth, vinegar, oil and mustard in a food processor or blender; blend until smooth.

Season with salt and pepper.

# Homemade Taco Seasoning

- 1 tablespoon chili powder
- ¼ teaspoon garlic powder
- ¼ teaspoon onion powder
- ¼ teaspoon crushed red pepper flakes
- ¼ teaspoon dried oregano
- ½ teaspoon paprika
- 1 ½ teaspoon ground cumin
- 1 teaspoon sea salt
- 1 teaspoon black pepper

Mix all ingredients together and store in an air tight container at room temp. 3-4 tablespoon of this seasoning easily replaces the store bought variety that often contains a lot more sodium.

- *6 tablespoon Olive Oil mayonnaise*
- *1 tablespoon lemon juice*
- *1 tablespoon vinegar*
- *1 tablespoon pepper*
- *1 Teaspoon sea salt*
- *1 teaspoon Splenda or Stevia*

Shake all ingredients together in a small jar.Lightly baste a thin layer on chicken just before removing from the grill.

This makes enough baste to use several times. Store remaining baste in refrigerator.

# Strawberry Jello

- 4½ cups apple juice (all-natural, no sugar added, 100% fruit juice)
- 1 tablespoon arrowroot
- ¼ cup agar flakes
- ⅛ teaspoon vanilla extract
- 3 cups fresh strawberries (about 12oz), quartered

Stir ½ cup of the juice and the arrowroot in a small bowl to blend; set aside. Combine the agar and salt with the remaining 4 cups juice in a heavy saucepan and bring to a simmer over high heat.

Decrease the heat to medium-low, cover and simmer, stirring frequently, for 15 minutes, or until the agar dissolves. Whisk in the arrowroot mixture. Cover and simmer, stirring occasionally, over medium-high heat for 5 minutes. Stir in the vanilla.

Transfer the jello to a large bowl and allow to cool at room temperature. When just beginning to set, gently stir in the strawberries. Spoon the jello into dessert bowls, cover, and refrigerate for 4 hours, or until set.

The jello will keep for 2 days, covered and refrigerated.

VARIATION: Try substituting blueberries or raspberries for the strawberries. You can also deepen the berry flavor by using an all-natural apple-berry juice.

- *12 oz. firm silken tofu*
- *2 tablespoons vinegar*
- *1 tablespoon olive oil*
- *1 teaspoon dry mustard*
- *¼ teaspoon minced garlic*
- *1 teaspoon dried dill*

Blend the tofu, vinegar, olive oil, mustard and garlic in a food processor until smooth. Transfer the sour cream to a container and stir in the dill.

Cover and refrigerate at least 2 hrs and up to 2 days.

# Shopping Guidelines

**Ketchup** - Heinz Reduced Sugar

**Mayonnaise** - Olive Oil Mayonnaise only, Kraft makes one

**Bragg Liquid Aminos** - tastes just like Soy Sauce but with way less sodium. Can be purchased at health food supermarkets or online

**BBQ Sauce** - Almost all BBQ sauces contain sugar as an ingredient. Look for one that advertises "Sugar Free" on the front label and then check the ingredients list on the back of the bottle to verify there are no sugars. Walden's Farm makes a Sugar Free BBQ Sauce

**Worcestershire Sauce** - Robbie's Worcestershire Sauce is sugar free and can be found at health food supermarkets or ordered online.

# Savings Coupon!

*Save when you help others!*

*Buy copies for your Challenge customers, team members or use as incentives! For a limited time, get bulk discounts with these discount coupon codes when you order direct from https://www.createspace.com/4032935*

## *FIVE OR MORE COPIES 33% OFF!*

1. Go to https://www.createspace.com/4032935 and click the 'Add to Cart' button
2. Change quantity to 5 or more & click 'Update Quantities'
3. Enter code: **9NNVSRJP** & click Apply Discount
4. Click Checkout - enter shipping & billing info

## *TEN OR MORE COPIES 50% OFF!*

1. Go to https://www.createspace.com/4032935 and click the 'Add to Cart' button
2. Change quantity to 10 or more & click 'Update Quantities'
3. Enter code: **LKUSGGFV** & click Apply Discount
4. Click Checkout - enter shipping & billing info

Made in the USA
Middletown, DE
29 December 2016